THIS
CHRISTMAS PLANNER
Belongs To:

_____

_____

_____

DEDICATION

This Christmas Planner is dedicated to all the busy people who want to organize and prepare in the months leading up to the holidays.

You are my inspiration for producing this book and I'm honored to be a part of your holiday planning.

HOW TO USE THIS BOOK

This Christmas Planner will help guide you through every detail of planning for the upcoming holiday season. Great for organizing all your activities and events.

Here are examples of information for you to fill in and write the details for your holiday planning.

Fill in the following information:

1. Happy Holidays Page- overview of holiday plans
2. Holiday Expense Tracker- date, description, category, amount
3. Christmas Budget Tracker- spending tracker, budget goal, actual spending, amount difference, budget ledger
4. November & December Planning Calendar
5. November & December Checklist Pages
6. Christmas Countdown Pages
7. Elf On The Shelf Planner
8. Holiday Playlist- band and artist music info
9. Holiday Movies To Watch Pages- record favorite movies & TV shows, rate favorite movies
10. Holiday Books To Read- plan your holiday reading and record title, author, and book review
11. Gift Ideas & Checklist- plan who the gift is for, gift idea, and store
12. Stocking Stuffer Ideas- write down ideas for 12 people
13. Holiday Wish List- record your list of items
14. Holiday Card Tracker Pages- space to record name and address
15. Christmas Planner Gift Pages- record recipients name, gift ideas, item description, store/website, and price
16. Black Friday, Cyber Monday, and Online Shopping Planner Pages- record store, item, discounts, and coupons
17. Cookie Baking List- plan cookie recipient list and delivery
18. Christmas Eve, Christmas, and New Years Eve Planning Pages- note pages for planning, meal planner, grocery list, checklist, holiday schedule with time slots, record holiday traditions
19. Gifts Received Pages
20. Holiday Gratitude Page- space to write what you are grateful for
21. Holiday Recipe Pages

Happy HOLIDAYS!

CHRISTMAS EVE PLANS

CHRISTMAS PLANS

NEW YEAR'S EVE PLANS

HOLIDAY *Expense Tracker*

DATE	DESCRIPTION	CATEGORY	AMOUNT

HOLIDAY Expense Tracker

DATE	DESCRIPTION	CATEGORY	AMOUNT

CHRISTMAS *Budget Tracker*

CHRISTMAS SPENDING TRACKER	
TOTAL BUDGET GOAL	
TOTAL ACTUAL SPENDING:	
DIFFERENCE	

CATEGORY	BUDGETED	ACTUAL COST	NOTES

CHRISTMAS *Budget Tracker*

CHRISTMAS SPENDING TRACKER	
TOTAL BUDGET GOAL	
TOTAL ACTUAL SPENDING:	
DIFFERENCE	

CATEGORY	BUDGETED	ACTUAL COST	NOTES

November Holiday PLANNING

M	T	W	T	F	S	S

- [ ]
- [ ]
- [ ]
- [ ]
- [ ]

December Holiday PLANNING

M	T	W	T	F	S	S

- [ ]
- [ ]
- [ ]
- [ ]
- [ ]

NOVEMBER HOLIDAY *Checklist*

DECEMBER HOLIDAY *Checklist*

Holiday PLANNING

Holiday PLANNING

13

14

15

16

17

18

19

20

21

22

23

24

ELF On The Shelf

ELF ANTICS	SUPPLIES NEEDED	DATE

HOLIDAY *Playlist*

ARTIST / BAND	SONG TITLE

HOLIDAY *Playlist*

ARTIST / BAND	SONG TITLE

HOLIDAY Movies to Watch

TOP CHRISTMAS MOVIES TO WATCH THIS SEASON

1   2   3   4   5

CHRISTMAS MOVIE IDEAS

CHRISTMAS TV SHOWS & SPECIALS

MOVIE TITLE   RATING ☆☆☆☆☆

DATE WATCHED:

MOVIE TITLE   RATING ☆☆☆☆☆

DATE WATCHED:

MOVIE TITLE   RATING ☆☆☆☆☆

DATE WATCHED:

MOVIE TITLE   RATING ☆☆☆☆☆

DATE WATCHED:

HOLIDAY *Movies to Watch*

TOP CHRISTMAS MOVIES TO WATCH THIS SEASON

1   2   3   4   5

CHRISTMAS MOVIE IDEAS

CHRISTMAS TV SHOWS & SPECIALS

MOVIE TITLE   **RATING** ☆☆☆☆☆

DATE WATCHED:

MOVIE TITLE   **RATING** ☆☆☆☆☆

DATE WATCHED:

MOVIE TITLE   **RATING** ☆☆☆☆☆

DATE WATCHED:

MOVIE TITLE   **RATING** ☆☆☆☆☆

DATE WATCHED:

HOLIDAY *Movies to Watch*

TOP CHRISTMAS MOVIES TO WATCH THIS SEASON

| 1 | 2 | 3 | 4 | 5 |

CHRISTMAS MOVIE IDEAS

CHRISTMAS TV SHOWS & SPECIALS

MOVIE TITLE RATING ☆☆☆☆☆

DATE WATCHED:

MOVIE TITLE RATING ☆☆☆☆☆

DATE WATCHED:

MOVIE TITLE RATING ☆☆☆☆☆

DATE WATCHED:

MOVIE TITLE RATING ☆☆☆☆☆

DATE WATCHED:

HOLIDAY *Movies to Watch*

TOP CHRISTMAS MOVIES TO WATCH THIS SEASON

1	2	3	4	5

CHRISTMAS MOVIE IDEAS

CHRISTMAS TV SHOWS & SPECIALS

MOVIE TITLE RATING ☆☆☆☆☆

DATE WATCHED:

MOVIE TITLE RATING ☆☆☆☆☆

DATE WATCHED:

MOVIE TITLE RATING ☆☆☆☆☆

DATE WATCHED:

MOVIE TITLE RATING ☆☆☆☆☆

DATE WATCHED:

HOLIDAY *Books to Read*

BOOK TITLE:

AUTHOR

START DATE:

PAGES

RATING ☆ ☆ ☆ ☆ ☆

MY BOOK REVIEW

OTHER BOOKS BY AUTHOR

HOLIDAY BOOK TO READ NEXT

HOLIDAY *Books to Read*

BOOK TITLE:

AUTHOR

START DATE:

PAGES

RATING ☆☆☆☆☆

MY BOOK REVIEW

OTHER BOOKS BY AUTHOR

HOLIDAY BOOK TO READ NEXT

GIFT IDEAS & Checklist

FOR: GIFT: STORE:

GIFT IDEAS & Checklist

FOR:	GIFT:	STORE:

GIFT IDEAS & Checklist

FOR:	GIFT:	STORE:

STOCKING *Stuffer Ideas*

NAME:

NAME:

NAME:

NAME:

NAME:

NAME:

STOCKING Stuffer Ideas

NAME:

NAME:

NAME:

NAME:

NAME:

NAME:

STOCKING Stuffer Ideas

NAME:

NAME:

NAME:

NAME:

NAME:

NAME:

HOLIDAY *Wish List*

ITEM	WANT	NEED
	○	○
	○	○
	○	○
	○	○
	○	○
	○	○
	○	○
	○	○
	○	○
	○	○
	○	○
	○	○
	○	○
	○	○
	○	○
	○	○
	○	○
	○	○
	○	○
	○	○
	○	○
	○	○
	○	○
	○	○
	○	○
	○	○

HOLIDAY *Wish List*

ITEM	WANT	NEED

HOLIDAY *Card Tracker*

NAME	ADDRESS	SENT

HOLIDAY *Card Tracker*

NAME	ADDRESS	SENT

HOLIDAY Card Tracker

NAME	ADDRESS	SENT

HOLIDAY Card Tracker

NAME	ADDRESS	SENT

HOLIDAY *Card Tracker*

NAME	ADDRESS	SENT

HOLIDAY *Card Tracker*

NAME	ADDRESS	SENT

HOLIDAY Card Tracker

NAME	ADDRESS	SENT

HOLIDAY Card Tracker

NAME	ADDRESS	SENT

CHRISTMAS *Gift Planner*

NAME	GIFT RECIPIENT		
	NOTES & IDEAS		

ITEM/DESCRIPTION	STORE/WEBSITE	PRICE

NAME	GIFT RECIPIENT		
	NOTES & IDEAS		

ITEM/DESCRIPTION	STORE/WEBSITE	PRICE

CHRISTMAS *Gift Planner*

NAME

GIFT RECIPIENT

NOTES & IDEAS

ITEM/DESCRIPTION	STORE/WEBSITE	PRICE

NAME

GIFT RECIPIENT

NOTES & IDEAS

ITEM/DESCRIPTION	STORE/WEBSITE	PRICE

CHRISTMAS *Gift Planner*

NAME	GIFT RECIPIENT		
	NOTES & IDEAS		

ITEM/DESCRIPTION	STORE/WEBSITE	PRICE

NAME	GIFT RECIPIENT		
	NOTES & IDEAS		

ITEM/DESCRIPTION	STORE/WEBSITE	PRICE

CHRISTMAS *Gift Planner*

	GIFT RECIPIENT
NAME	NOTES & IDEAS

ITEM/DESCRIPTION	STORE/WEBSITE	PRICE

	GIFT RECIPIENT
NAME	NOTES & IDEAS

ITEM/DESCRIPTION	STORE/WEBSITE	PRICE

CHRISTMAS *Gift Planner*

NAME

GIFT RECIPIENT

NOTES & IDEAS

ITEM/DESCRIPTION	STORE/WEBSITE	PRICE

NAME

GIFT RECIPIENT

NOTES & IDEAS

ITEM/DESCRIPTION	STORE/WEBSITE	PRICE

CHRISTMAS Gift Planner

NAME	GIFT RECIPIENT
	NOTES & IDEAS

ITEM/DESCRIPTION	STORE/WEBSITE	PRICE

NAME	GIFT RECIPIENT
	NOTES & IDEAS

ITEM/DESCRIPTION	STORE/WEBSITE	PRICE

CHRISTMAS *Gift Planner*

NAME	GIFT RECIPIENT		
	NOTES & IDEAS		

ITEM/DESCRIPTION	STORE/WEBSITE	PRICE

NAME	GIFT RECIPIENT		
	NOTES & IDEAS		

ITEM/DESCRIPTION	STORE/WEBSITE	PRICE

CHRISTMAS *Gift Planner*

NAME	GIFT RECIPIENT
	NOTES & IDEAS

ITEM/DESCRIPTION	STORE/WEBSITE	PRICE

NAME	GIFT RECIPIENT
	NOTES & IDEAS

ITEM/DESCRIPTION	STORE/WEBSITE	PRICE

CHRISTMAS *Gift Planner*

NAME	GIFT RECIPIENT	
	NOTES & IDEAS	

ITEM/DESCRIPTION	STORE/WEBSITE	PRICE

NAME	GIFT RECIPIENT	
	NOTES & IDEAS	

ITEM/DESCRIPTION	STORE/WEBSITE	PRICE

CHRISTMAS *Gift Planner*

NAME	GIFT RECIPIENT
	NOTES & IDEAS

ITEM/DESCRIPTION	STORE/WEBSITE	PRICE

NAME	GIFT RECIPIENT
	NOTES & IDEAS

ITEM/DESCRIPTION	STORE/WEBSITE	PRICE

CHRISTMAS *Gift Planner*

NAME	GIFT RECIPIENT
	NOTES & IDEAS

ITEM/DESCRIPTION	STORE/WEBSITE	PRICE

NAME	GIFT RECIPIENT
	NOTES & IDEAS

ITEM/DESCRIPTION	STORE/WEBSITE	PRICE

CHRISTMAS *Gift Planner*

NAME

GIFT RECIPIENT

NOTES & IDEAS

ITEM/DESCRIPTION	STORE/WEBSITE	PRICE

NAME

GIFT RECIPIENT

NOTES & IDEAS

ITEM/DESCRIPTION	STORE/WEBSITE	PRICE

CHRISTMAS *Gift Planner*

| NAME | GIFT RECIPIENT |
| | NOTES & IDEAS |

ITEM/DESCRIPTION	STORE/WEBSITE	PRICE

| NAME | GIFT RECIPIENT |
| | NOTES & IDEAS |

ITEM/DESCRIPTION	STORE/WEBSITE	PRICE

CHRISTMAS *Gift Planner*

NAME	GIFT RECIPIENT		
	NOTES & IDEAS		

ITEM/DESCRIPTION	STORE/WEBSITE	PRICE

NAME	GIFT RECIPIENT		
	NOTES & IDEAS		

ITEM/DESCRIPTION	STORE/WEBSITE	PRICE

CHRISTMAS *Gift Planner*

NAME

GIFT RECIPIENT

NOTES & IDEAS

ITEM/DESCRIPTION	STORE/WEBSITE	PRICE

NAME

GIFT RECIPIENT

NOTES & IDEAS

ITEM/DESCRIPTION	STORE/WEBSITE	PRICE

CHRISTMAS *Gift Planner*

NAME	GIFT RECIPIENT		
	NOTES & IDEAS		

ITEM/DESCRIPTION	STORE/WEBSITE	PRICE

NAME	GIFT RECIPIENT		
	NOTES & IDEAS		

ITEM/DESCRIPTION	STORE/WEBSITE	PRICE

CHRISTMAS *Gift Planner*

NAME	GIFT RECIPIENT
	NOTES & IDEAS

ITEM/DESCRIPTION	STORE/WEBSITE	PRICE

NAME	GIFT RECIPIENT
	NOTES & IDEAS

ITEM/DESCRIPTION	STORE/WEBSITE	PRICE

CHRISTMAS *Gift Planner*

NAME	GIFT RECIPIENT
	NOTES & IDEAS

ITEM/DESCRIPTION	STORE/WEBSITE	PRICE

NAME	GIFT RECIPIENT
	NOTES & IDEAS

ITEM/DESCRIPTION	STORE/WEBSITE	PRICE

CHRISTMAS *Gift Planner*

NAME

GIFT RECIPIENT

NOTES & IDEAS

ITEM/DESCRIPTION	STORE/WEBSITE	PRICE

NAME

GIFT RECIPIENT

NOTES & IDEAS

ITEM/DESCRIPTION	STORE/WEBSITE	PRICE

CHRISTMAS Gift Planner

NAME

GIFT RECIPIENT

NOTES & IDEAS

ITEM/DESCRIPTION	STORE/WEBSITE	PRICE

NAME

GIFT RECIPIENT

NOTES & IDEAS

ITEM/DESCRIPTION	STORE/WEBSITE	PRICE

Black Friday SHOPPING

STORE	ITEM	COUPON	DISCOUNT

Black Friday SHOPPING

STORE	ITEM	COUPON	DISCOUNT

Cyber Monday SHOPPING

STORE	ITEM	COUPON	DISCOUNT

Cyber Monday SHOPPING

STORE	ITEM	COUPON	DISCOUNT

Online SHOPPING

STORE	ITEM	COUPON	DISCOUNT

Online SHOPPING

STORE	ITEM	COUPON	DISCOUNT

COOKIE BAKING *List*

COOKIES FOR	DELIVERED

COOKIE BAKING *List*

COOKIES FOR	DELIVERED

Christmas Eve PLANNING

CHRISTMAS EVE MEAL *Planner*

STARTERS/APPS

MAIN DISHES

SIDE DISHES

BEVERAGES

DESSERTS

Other Ideas

CHRISTMAS EVE *Grocery List*

CHRISTMAS EVE *Checklist*

Christmas Eve SCHEDULE

HOLIDAY SCHEDULE

7 AM	4 PM
8 AM	5 PM
9 AM	6 PM
10 AM	7 PM
11 AM	8 PM
12 PM	9 PM
1 PM	10 PM
2 PM	11 PM
3 PM	12 PM

NOTES & REMINDERS

CHRISTMAS EVE *Traditions*

Christmas Eve Tradition:

Christmas Eve Tradition:

Christmas Eve Tradition:

CHRISTMAS EVE *Traditions*

Christmas Eve Tradition:

Christmas Eve Tradition:

Christmas Eve Tradition:

Christmas PLANNING

25

CHRISTMAS MEAL *Planner*

STARTERS/APPS

MAIN DISHES

SIDE DISHES

BEVERAGES

DESSERTS

Other Ideas

CHRISTMAS *Grocery List*

CHRISTMAS *Checklist*

Christmas SCHEDULE

HOLIDAY SCHEDULE

7 AM

8 AM

9 AM

10 AM

11 AM

12 PM

1 PM

2 PM

3 PM

4 PM

5 PM

6 PM

7 PM

8 PM

9 PM

10 PM

11 PM

12 PM

NOTES & REMINDERS

CHRISTMAS Traditions

Christmas Tradition:

Christmas Tradition:

Christmas Tradition:

CHRISTMAS *Traditions*

Christmas Tradition:

Christmas Tradition:

Christmas Tradition:

GIFTS Received

FROM	ITEM

GIFTS *Received*

FROM	ITEM

HOLIDAY *Gratitude*

What I am grateful for:

CHRISTMAS
is the spirit of
giving
without a thought of getting

New Year's Eve PLANNING

NEW YEAR'S EVE *Planner*

STARTERS/APPS

MAIN DISHES

SIDE DISHES

BEVERAGES

DESSERTS

Other Ideas

NEW YEAR'S EVE *Grocery List*

NEW YEAR'S EVE *Checklist*

New Year's Eve SCHEDULE

HOLIDAY SCHEDULE

7 AM

8 AM

9 AM

10 AM

11 AM

12 PM

1 PM

2 PM

3 PM

4 PM

5 PM

6 PM

7 PM

8 PM

9 PM

10 PM

11 PM

12 PM

NOTES & REMINDERS

NEW YEAR'S EVE *Traditions*

New Year's Eve Tradition:

New Year's Eve Tradition:

New Year's Eve Tradition:

NEW YEAR'S EVE *Traditions*

New Year's Eve Tradition:

New Year's Eve Tradition:

New Year's Eve Tradition:

HOLIDAY *Recipes*

RECIPE TITLE

SOURCE

OVEN TEMPERATURE

INGREDIENTS

DIRECTIONS

HOLIDAY *Recipes*

RECIPE TITLE

SOURCE

OVEN TEMPERATURE

INGREDIENTS

DIRECTIONS

HOLIDAY *Recipes*

RECIPE TITLE

SOURCE

OVEN TEMPERATURE

INGREDIENTS

DIRECTIONS

HOLIDAY *Recipes*

RECIPE TITLE

SOURCE

OVEN TEMPERATURE

INGREDIENTS

DIRECTIONS

HOLIDAY *Recipes*

RECIPE TITLE

SOURCE

OVEN TEMPERATURE

INGREDIENTS

DIRECTIONS

HOLIDAY *Recipes*

RECIPE TITLE

SOURCE

OVEN TEMPERATURE

INGREDIENTS

DIRECTIONS

HOLIDAY *Recipes*

RECIPE TITLE

SOURCE

OVEN TEMPERATURE

INGREDIENTS

DIRECTIONS

HOLIDAY *Recipes*

RECIPE TITLE

SOURCE

OVEN TEMPERATURE

INGREDIENTS

DIRECTIONS

HOLIDAY *Recipes*

RECIPE TITLE

SOURCE

OVEN TEMPERATURE

INGREDIENTS

DIRECTIONS

HOLIDAY *Recipes*

RECIPE TITLE

SOURCE

OVEN TEMPERATURE

INGREDIENTS

DIRECTIONS

HOLIDAY *Recipes*

RECIPE TITLE

SOURCE

OVEN TEMPERATURE

INGREDIENTS

DIRECTIONS

HOLIDAY *Recipes*

RECIPE TITLE

SOURCE

OVEN TEMPERATURE

INGREDIENTS

DIRECTIONS

HOLIDAY *Recipes*

RECIPE TITLE

SOURCE

OVEN TEMPERATURE

INGREDIENTS

DIRECTIONS

HOLIDAY *Recipes*

RECIPE TITLE

SOURCE

OVEN TEMPERATURE

INGREDIENTS

DIRECTIONS

HOLIDAY *Recipes*

RECIPE TITLE   SOURCE

OVEN TEMPERATURE

INGREDIENTS

DIRECTIONS

HOLIDAY *Recipes*

RECIPE TITLE

SOURCE

OVEN TEMPERATURE

INGREDIENTS

DIRECTIONS

HOLIDAY Recipes

RECIPE TITLE

SOURCE

OVEN TEMPERATURE

INGREDIENTS

DIRECTIONS

HOLIDAY *Recipes*

RECIPE TITLE

SOURCE

OVEN TEMPERATURE

INGREDIENTS

DIRECTIONS

HOLIDAY *Recipes*

RECIPE TITLE   SOURCE

OVEN TEMPERATURE

INGREDIENTS

DIRECTIONS

CPSIA information can be obtained
at www.ICGtesting.com
Printed in the USA
LVHW112000051121
702532LV00016BA/1202

9 781953 557353